SATYR'S WIFE

Poems

by

Rita Signorelli-Pappas

SERVING HOUSE BOOKS

Satyr's Wife

Copyright © 2009 Rita Signorelli-Pappas

Cover photo by Stephen Lawrence

Author photo by Alan Shaw

ISBN: 978-0-9825462-5-3

Serving House Books logo by Barry Lereng Wilmont

Published by Serving House Books

www.servinghousebooks.com

First Edition

For John, Sarah, and James Pappas,
and for Stephen Lawrence

Acknowledgments

Some of these poems originally appeared in the following publications, to whose editors grateful acknowledgment is made:

College English: "Riding with Keats," "A Sister's Wedding," "Black Coat"
Kansas Quarterly: "Basket of Oranges"
The Literary Review: "The Ghost of Tintoretto's Daughter," "Reading at Silvacane," "Pythia: The Process" (reprinted in *Verse Daily*)
Northeast Corridor: "Petunias"
Notre Dame Review: "I Run into Count Ugolino," "Mind Clearing in a Chinese Landscape"
New Orleans Review: "Arachne" (reprinted in *Poetry Daily*), "Already Autumn"
The Plum Review: "Moths"
Poet Lore: "Medusa"
Poetry: "Beautiful Girl Café," "Hunger Artist"
Poetry Northwest: "Ariel"
Prairie Schooner: "Semele," "The Road to Sénanque," "Ariadne in Verona," "Sister-in-law," "On the Appian Way"
River Styx: "After Abstinence"
Shenandoah: "Tereus and Philomel," "Apollo and Daphne"
Southern Humanities Review: "Venice"
Southern Poetry Review: "Folktale"
Southwest Review: "Mushrooms"
Tampa Review: "Satyr's Wife"

The Women's Review of Books: "*Sati*/Widow Burning,"
  "Judith Visits the Past," "The Nuns of Alba"
Valparaiso Poetry Review: "Parmigianino Thinking"

Rita Signorelli-Pappas has been writing and publishing poetry for over twenty years. Her poems have appeared in *Poetry, Shenandoah, Poetry Northwest, Southwest Review, Prairie Schooner, Southern Poetry Review, Chelsea, The Literary Review,* and *Poet Lore,* among other journals. Her poetry has also appeared on the websites *Verse Daily* and *Poetry Daily.* A Pushcart Prize nominee, she was a finalist for the 2008 May Swenson Award, and she received the 2008 Italian Americana Award in Fiction.

She has taught courses in writing and literature at Valparaiso University and Purdue University. Her degrees include a B.A. from Douglass College and an M.A. in Italian literature from Rutgers University. She has been a regular reviewer for *Small Press Review* and *The Women's Review of Books,* and she currently reviews poetry for *World Literature Today.*

Contents

Introduction

The poems in *Satyr's Wife* call up worlds gained through travel or reading: Italy, China, mythic time, the consciousness of Keats. Wherever the poem goes, a literal landscape or a text, there's an urgency to the way it moves, as if the voice is looking for something it might die without. The writer and literary scholar Richard Maxwell, who has sometimes taught Rita Signorelli-Pappas's poems, has a nice analysis. These poems "seem at first to inhabit familiar cultural landmarks: Ovidian myth, Venice, the Appian Way, a still-life by Matisse. But understatement and delicacy of touch release a transformative power. These lyrics appropriate myth or Matisse with a smooth, almost insidious thoroughness, then subtly change direction; indeed, there is always one more shift, at least, than the reader has anticipated. And some of the endings have a wonderful way of negating everything that has come before, while seeming to propose, to bring into being, a whole new poem, one that we are just now prepared to read."

Those surprising shifts in direction are, I think, what makes these poems retain their mystery. I love the way Pappas so viscerally absorbs herself in her material and then subverts the narrative somehow, either with a jump from Ovid's time to ours: "Somewhere white eagles rush down / like searchlights through the pines," or through female-centered perspectives, as in the hypnotic and erotic "Apollo and Daphne," or in these lines from "Arachne,": "or it might have been / the slow hand of Zeus travelling a woman's body and / when she finally emerged from the long tunnel of silk / she saw that her own body hung exposed / in a shimmering web she was dead no she was alive."

Pappas's work has the lush intensity of poems by Sylvia Plath or Louise Glück, but her vision is particularly hers—gorgeous, but never merely so—there's a hard precision and even a brutal turn to some of the passages I admire most as in, "Moths": At noon new griefs / hung in the window shade / like the shadows of a thousand bees / that dissolved into a crimson cloud, / then came back to bead my mirror / with a sudden mist of blood."

Maybe all poets are in exile, living as they do in these alternate terrains made of words. But I think of the poet Rita Signorelli-Pappas as writing from a particular site of displacement. An east coast native who spent her early life in various New Jersey cities (and who now lives in Princeton), she lived and wrote for two decades in semi-rural Valparaiso, Indiana—a place with white-out, icy winters, a hearty tradition of popcorn festivals and basketball fandom, and the town motto "Vale of Paradise." That's where we became friends, so I'm glad she landed there, but especially because for Rita, though it might not be an obviously literary or exotic setting, it turned out to be a great place to write. There was the university library, and there were those long winters, when one might look up from the desk out the window and see nothing but thick snow, like another clean sheet of paper.

There's only a little of that literal landscape in the poems here, as in "I run into Count Ugolino on the autumn day when / I finally start scraping frost from my windshield." ("I Run Into Count Ugolino"). The speaker is driving to Indianapolis with Dante, who has become a scholar now, "writing an impassioned essay on the émigré poet / that he will read at 2 o'clock this afternoon / in a hotel ballroom somewhere in the city." Dante's creation, Count Ugolino, is also in the car, blithely off and on gnawing on Ruggiero's head. In *The Inferno*, the Count is trapped in ice up to his neck, stuck in the ninth circle of hell for treason, doomed to cannibalize the head of his betrayer. In her typical (and fascinating) fashion, Pappas doesn't refer to this hell-ice directly in the poem, allowing the allusion to emerge from the landscape. And the Count's chewing on the head is treated with black humor, not horror, until the poem masterfully juxtaposes a more ruminative tone against the joking asides. The Count's consuming of the head starts to seem industrious—he nibbles on a pencil, linking his voraciousness to writing. At the end of the poem, the speaker channels both Dante and the Count. She may be trapped in this wintry landscape, but with a wild and ravenous mind:

It goes on—the deep longing / for thought, the wind's feverish reverie as it strips / the orchard of leaves. It goes on—the rumination of memory, / the mind's profusion caught in a rubbing click and chirr. / It happens over and over. The way the eyes begin / to narrow. The snap of jaws starting to work.

Most of these poems have been previously published in literary magazines, and it's wonderful to finally have them gathered together in the collection *Satyr's Wife*, which I hope will find many more readers. Rita Signorelli-Pappas's poems not only seduce one into reading and re-reading, but they give the act of writing a new radiance:

I sat at the table to shape
these dark, fading syllables,
this black salt tossed into
the empty cauldron of spring.

—René Steinke

Arachne

The belled air ringing.
Slowly she wakes through a craving
to weave, through a sunlit dream
of Athena singing her back into sleep,
she is alive no she is dead and it is Athena
standing watch over the ghost of her human form,
Athena who undid the plaited rope until it was
only a single strand and then she floated into
another way of moving so soft that she felt
her entire body whirled through a maze of light
and then her body disappeared and for a moment
she drowsed inside her shadow and then it was Athena
who told her what she had become or else
it was the mouth of an Argive woman speaking
after she had devoured her infant or perhaps
it was the eyes of Teiresias watching two snakes
coupling in the grass or it might have been
the slow hand of Zeus traveling a woman's body and
when she finally emerged from the long tunnel of silk
she saw that her own body hung exposed
in a shimmering web she was dead no she was alive
her skin reeling bright silver filaments helplessly
into the dusk. There was nothing else to feel
but a terrible hunger to spin.

Beautiful Girl Café

—For John

At dusk while we sat and talked
in our Beautiful Girl Café
across from the Pitti Palace
your imagination practiced loving
that tall, virginal waitress
serving us cups of lemon tea.

When she left our table
your temples rustled with
a delicate wreath of pine,
and when she drifted through
the airy garden behind the bar
your breathless body followed
on a pair of goat feet.

Call this a twilight fable
but I heard jeweled hooves
chiming on the courtyard tiles.
I saw your face grown innocent
when you returned, your gray hair
tossing like broken reeds.

Satyr's Wife

I wanted to be the satyr's wild wife.

I used to stalk him through the forest
amazed by his hoofbeats of blue thunder,
the silver tail flashing like a lightning bolt.
That forehead crowned with musky horns.

He had the strange, sleety gaze
of whirlwinds in darkness.

I followed him to watch the way
he flicked a reed pipe to his lips
and blew music that would flush
the crazed boar from hiding.

Somewhere white eagles rush down
like searchlights through the pines—
that is how my dream of the satyr
came to me. I would suddenly see myself
suckling a horned infant
under red willow trees by a river.
And I would feel the satyr's eyes
on me like a knife.

Now my life is that dream.
The satyr pipes his brutal notes

in the blood-haze of these willows
while his moody infant dozes at my breast.
His music surrounds me with
madness, catastrophe, and smoke.

I want to be a bubble of air
rising in the dead river.

I Run into Count Ugolino

I run into Count Ugolino on the autumn day when
I finally start scraping frost from my windshield.
It's destiny, this meeting—we've been
avoiding it for years. I'm proud of the way
I maintain my composure, glad that Dante
is standing beside me, glad that the crazed Count
has finally stopped gnawing Ruggieri's head.
"Quite a meal!" I comment dryly to Dante and he gives
a feeling nod. I toss Ruggieri's skull into the trunk,
then we all pile into my car and take
the back road to Indianapolis so we can admire
the abandoned trees tossing in their jazzy silks.
Ugolino needs a break, and his creator looks as if
he could use some fresh inspiration. I don't mind
when the poet lights up his pipe, but I keep
an uneasy eye on the Count's jittery hands. If this
were Rome, we'd drive to the Baths of Caracalla,
find a steamroom where our exhausted bodies
would disrobe and be anointed with the sweetness
of wax and oil. We're all so tired, it seems
to happen in October—that hiss of sadness
whenever the icy wind hits Lake Michigan's
scalding waves. I worry when Ugolino shifts in his seat
to sit on his hands, I'm frantic to break
the silence but I let Dante do it for me—he's
writing an impassioned essay on the émigré poet
that he will read at two o'clock this afternoon

in a hotel ballroom somewhere in the city.
He's headed for a life of scholarship now that
the poetry well is dry. I remember the artist
who had to kill herself one day in a bathtub
when her paintings were no longer a solace,
I imagine the hushed tongue of her paintbrush,
the new canvas whitening into a sea of smoke.
I know how Ugolino's wild eyes stared into the
ice fog that came rolling over his tower window—
when it lifted there was only a frostwork of
thin blue hieroglyphs spinning on the glass.
By the time we turn off for lunch, Dante
is scribbling furiously at his clipboard and
the Count's brutal mouth is nibbling a pencil—
I'm not hungry, I just want to fly into the red mist
of a mountain ash and tear at the bitter berries with my teeth.
Instead I freeze when the trunk key turns in its lock
and I see the Count grinding at Ruggieri like a dog.
Back on the road, Dante reads us his final draft—
he is speaking and weeping all the way into the city,
he goes on right up to the hotel door. Ugolino wipes
his mouth on Ruggieri's hair and mutely waves goodbye.
I leave them both lost in contemplation outside
the Marriott. Why does it always happen in the fall,
this wanting to walk every field of rosy stubble
with Dante or Keats? It goes on—the deep longing
for thought, the wind's feverish reverie as it strips
the orchard of leaves. It goes on—the rumination of memory,
the mind's profusion caught in a rubbing click and chirr.
It happens over and over. The way the eyes begin
to narrow. The snap of jaws starting to work.

Folktale

A woman from Castelvetrano
used to grow roses with
a scent so strong and wild
it still rises in my nostrils
whenever a cloud passes the moon
and pulls sadness down over me
like a veil of black netting.

She hid fish teeth in a jar
of cracked glass, scrambled my eggs
in thick, green oil and the night
her daughter died I watched her
bite a cold wax apple.

She came from a dusty old village
in Sicily, that place where
the bones of lost white mules
sing in the mountains, and oh
I watched her choose her steps
slowly coming down the ruined
trails of this life. Sometimes
her death finds me like a sleepwalker,
lifts the veil from my face
and kisses me on the eyes.

Hunger Artist

I believe I could have saved him.
What he wanted was easy: the poured
sweet wine of encouragement. A smile.

In another life he might have grown
a comfortable margin of flesh, he might
have kept all his teeth and been spared

translation into the skeleton's cage.
I would have kept an eye on him,
fed him with words passed like bread

broken into a confession of trust.
I would have revealed my own fast,
my own body ribboned into syllables

of bone. I would have untied
the sad bow of his mouth
looped and knotted for a kiss.

Riding with Keats

He is so light that his patient horse
might carry him for a thousand years,
this little man whose hand
clutches quietly at the reins.
When we ride each morning
along the Tiber, I see
the ardor of his bowed face
flash over the dark water.
I watch his eyes that watch nothing
glow and deepen with
the slow immensity of words,
I feel his whole body grow
into another language,
the sweet and awkward syllables
of its solitude.

Our horses' nostrils quiver
with each quick breath of rising wind
as if they smelled the coming snow.

But what will come with the snow?

The storm of a thousand hooves
plunging across the piazza,
the ghostly hailstones chiming
in a dazzle of blue crystal

under our stunned feet,
the sudden hush of deep drifts
closing endlessly over the loneliness
of our long ride together
through this hardbreathing silence.

Medusa

The power to fix, the power to freeze—
she never wanted it—

the row of sweat beads licked from her brow
by a hovering tongue and

too many eyes, too many mouths,
the dizzy slide of a thousand purple scales,

the pale blink of albino eyelids,
one throat opening up to swallow another

or the blind flash of her own tongue
flicking raindrops off her skin

while the hands of childhood continue their dream
weaving her hair into a soft familiar braid,

time's perpetual vibrations, one day taken
into another with a bold, slow-moving ease,

the sinuous soul floating out from its snakehook
toward a glimpse of the faraway,

swaying, always swaying to the charmed rhythms
of a private fever,

but her eyes crave focus,
her mind cannot lose

the desire to encapsulate images,
the power to choose a picture of life

and make it hold.
The way out. The mastery of pain.

Petunias

Lately
I've come to study
the lush, blazing
bodies of their tenderness

as if they were
the anatomy of rapture,
I've been listening when
their soundless music

lightens the air with
a profusion of notes
silky and delicate
as a pulse. Whenever

the sun tilts,
the ardent funnels of their faces
humbly lift and fill
with an unstoppable light.

I keep watching them.
I keep asking myself
what I know about
devotion in this life.

I follow their gaze into
the sky's amphitheater
to memorize
the revelation of clouds.

The day goes slowly dark and wild
but petunias
raise their pitchers and pour
a fire of kindness.

A Sister's Wedding

I have vowed to stay patient so now
on the day of your wedding
I deny you nothing. Even when
you raise the serious gun of your
makeup brush my eyes blink yes.
I want to let you begin all over
if only for today. I want to wear
the strong gypsy blush of your face,
to swoon into the nighthawk stare
of your bold, frightened longing.
You pass the cool wand over my lids
and I am blinded by the flash
of our cruel, ardent sisterhood,
the shudder of love's hot heartbeat
as it locks and starts to fail.
Your frail, yearning shoulders
lean forward as you begin to pummel
my cheeks with hungry pink dust.
Look, you say, smiling, and turn
my shoulders until they almost touch
the mirror that has us surrounded.
And as I watch I think how it took
forty years to lead us to this one
dissolving moment when we seek
each other's painted face in the glass
and find only a wild clear silence,
a cold smoke of bridal lace.

Tereus and Philomel

When he was finished with her,
when he lay sated on top of her,
her mouth bleeding into his hair,
when he had pinned her hands above her head
and taken her over and over
in the terrible silence, when he had
finally made her used to the way
lust could blunt and freeze the soul,

when he was through with her,
when moonlight bounded softly into the room
like the ghost of a white wolf,
when he saw the quiet hatred for him
moving in her eyes, when he had yawned
and rolled the brutal weight of himself
off her body, only then did he hear

the dazed sparks hissing and twittering in the air,
the wordless ephemera of a voice
growing louder and louder
as it seethed and broke like
molten bubbles inside his nerves
already wounded into wildness.

Already Autumn

It was already autumn and there were too many
red and yellow leaves, too many secrets,
silences and averted eyes, that was the autumn
when shadows of herons slid over our house and the air
would darken and smell of smoke, it was the autumn
I stopped sleeping because of a friend's suicide and
the departure of a son, I just kept my eyes lowered and hardly
moved, like a heron skating slowly through the water
for there were days when the smoke thickened
as I remembered the revolt of Absalom whose
father blew him a kiss and left him the kingdom
which is why I wove a set of pipes from broken reeds
and wandered the wood of Ephraim every night
playing the music of wisdom and sorrow softly
the way my friend's eyes closed as she leaned into the water,
the way the raptor glided down into our yard,
the way you drifted into other rooms all autumn
which was how you stood watch over my desperation,
but in the end it was the crows who saved me
with their ruined geniality and clumsy bows,
their brooding improvisations with twigs and string
to prepare for the years of soulful darkness oh I started
to believe again in gusto I followed the gypsy
dream-lift of their bodies whenever the curtain
of air swung open and they flew for their lives
straight through the black branches into a world
of devotion and plunder oh Absalom my son.

Moths

1.

Every night I imagined them
weaving ghost galleries in the trees,
their pale wings rustling
like sails of angelsmoke,
their dusty silhouettes fluttering
around the lantern of the moon.

2.

At noon new griefs
hung in the window shade
like the shadows of a thousand bees
that dissolved into a crimson cloud,
then came back to bead my mirror
with a sudden mist of blood.

3.

Images haunted me, flying out of sight
only to return—moments when
the folded bodies of moths
floated like kites
at the ends of silken cords
in a windy dusk.

4.

I did not rise at sunset
to twirl down paths of air,
I did not dine on nectar,
I could not tear what I knew
of lust and death from my shoulders
like a strand of broken pearls.

5.

In a white, bare tundra
the antennae of moths
quivered like feathers of ice.
And layer by layer, imagination
wove for me its golden cave of exile
fastened to a branch of thorn.

6.

Betrayals stalked me. I wore them
alone in drafty cathedrals
like gowns of bitter incense,
I wore them through smoking deserts,
their ghosts swept through me
with the force of deadly winds.

7.

The slow hands of meditation
plucked me like a mandolin.
My visions painted themselves
into fiery red eyes
that glowed and blinked
on the torn wings of moths.

Ariel

The gray trunk shudders
   and splits.
A pale form appears.
   He flicks the scented
shards of pine bark
   from his hair,
sips air as strange
   and spiced as
chameleon's breath.
   He wonders
whom to thank
   for this piquant
splash of freedom.
   Will it disappear
by midday? dusk?
   When his face
starts to rise from
   the near river's glass
he wonders if
   he still has eyes
but there they are—
   two quick, bright
fever flashes.
   Now the sudden taste
of resin
   in his mouth—

the memory of five thousand
    nights and days
branched and rooted
    in a cold cathedral
of blue pine.
    Cliffs stand about
like druids,
    sandhills whimper
and shift. Is
    all this his?
Whenever the maddened
    organ cries of wind
begin to weep
    and rise toward heaven,
he stops to listen.
    Then a form appears.
Is it God, this body
    moving like
a waterfall of light?
    This deft, dangerous hand
that touches him
    like a mother?

Venice

Singing woke me.
There were sounds of unknown voices in the street.
A boat was passing on the canal.
A porcelain mask lay on the table.

The cantata was by Scarlatti.
The voices echoed from the Carnival.
Because you left on that passing boat
I did not place the mask over my face

or cross the bridge of Istrian stone
as cool and white as your body.
I did not enter the sea-scented palace
hung with glistening tapestries of swans.

Instead I saw doves thicken in the square
and then the air began to form
its first hushed gestures of snow
like a slow, eerie mime.

When the swift flakes were falling,
when there were too many wounds to be grasped,
when April was just another small gray coal
left to crumble inside the heart

I sat at the table to shape
these dark, fading syllables,
this black salt tossed into
the empty cauldron of spring.

The Ghost of Tintoretto's Daughter

When you returned from Venice you had changed,
we were no longer comrades—I saw that right away.
The moon kept its old devoted deathwatch
all the way home from the airport
but you hardly noticed, you barely spoke.

So I had to imagine every lovesick vignette—
how scarves of shimmering mist from the lagoon
drifted up your back-alley window
like a courtesan's winding yellow veil,
how you woke with hands that had grown
thick and strange as a sphinx's paws,
then at noon you crossed the weathered square
to enter a bookshop. It must have been there that
you met her—the ghost of Tintoretto's daughter.

She was wearing black trousers and a tie,
she was smoking a cigarette as she searched
the tightly packed shelves of books.
When you asked what she was looking for,
she swept the straight blueblack hair from her eyes
and murmured, "Oh, just some light reading."
What could you do but shiver and be seduced?

In a daze you followed her up and down the aisles.
As she browsed the volumes of feminist thought
a shock seemed to pass through her body.

Not everyone knew that she too was an artist.
Not everyone knew that most of the paintings
in her father's name were done by her own hand.
It was he who made her dress like this,
he thought he owned her—even when she married
he made her promise never to leave his house.

Her hair had fallen once again into her eyes.
Outside it began to rain. Would her father
explode the silence like a thunderbolt,
seize her arm, and lead her back to his workshop?
A sudden downdraft scoured the room.
You reached up to close a slamming shutter
but when you turned around she was gone.

Through the open door you saw a streetlight
glittering in the fog and you followed it.
Racing over the stone bridges, you called her name—
you rushed up and down the narrow lanes
hoping for one more glimpse of her.

But the city stayed just as it was.
The canals gave off their scent of must and brine.
A child rolled a hoop across your path
humming snatches of a carnival tune.
The wind worked you over like a wild masseuse
pummeling your body with ashes and oil.
Finally your steps faltered and you lost your way.

Now, something in your tone gives me notice.
This car recedes and we become two figures
rowing a gondola down the Grand Canal.

Our boat glows silver in the moonlight.
Our only passenger has blueblack hair
that keeps falling lightly into her eyes.
She wears dark trousers and a tie and as
she strums the silk strings of a lute,
I can hear her singing softly to herself
words that will haunt our nights like stars
and take us far into the loneliness of life
where the dead are not the dead.

Sati/Widow Burning

Sing on in your distant snow
with the fire's tower glittering
your despair stitched and knotted
in my linen heart

The air churns such clouds
of rough burning sand your words
weave themselves through my body
this cool emaciation of flower roots

Sing to me with a satyr's voice
Gentle me with an executioner's hand
as your body smokes before me
like the purity of prayer

How the hushed flames watch me
with a wild oracular stare
now that I am finally here with you
black pearl in my mouth

Semele

Dusk leaning into night
the moon's weedy nest glows
in a tree of stars
in the darkness of his lair
she sleeps and dreams
he comes to her as fire
the sequined air whirls
hot kisses test her lips
there is the shock of sparks
flung like arms around her waist
a wild sweet terrifying
taste of flame in her mouth
now her soul ignites
weightless and finally free
the bold fingers of light
rush to please her
smoke rises through floodlit
branches of sky and now
she feels herself both
sun and moon the fire
has opened her forever
her body blooms
white and intelligible
among glittering leaves.

Apollo and Daphne

so she turned and he watched
her brow vanish her hair
rippling into leaves now his
fingers could almost touch her in
the haze of wind and mossy light
and her warm white skin cooled
to a smoke of brown and green
as he heard felt saw her breathing
stop as he imagined the first faint
gesture of her yes this was not
supposed to happen to a god this
straining for the sounds of whispers
through a tumbling mist while
the silence disembodied her and
pulled another form out of the air
a silhouette of scarves and wands
chiming rustling so he knew
she could breathe again he saw
her body lean forward in
a slim dainty sheath of bark
and when he put his ear to
the trunk of her chest he could
hear the wild beating of her
hunted animal heart yes he was
finally holding her yes he could feel
her branches sway he could see
the glowing treetop of her head

slowly nodding yes he was only a god
yes she could feel his need she would
stand watch forever over his life this
was the devotion he had dreamed of
her dappled arms enfolding him
green speaking shadows

For the Sibyl

It may be that was a kind of praying when
I hid out in the woods alone even in the rain
or maybe that was the way bitterness began
when I tore the buds off the honeysuckles
with my teeth although it was decades before
the mouths inside the cave started speaking
and centuries after the anchorites in the desert
hypnotized themselves with whispering and weaving

so maybe that was how I learned to live in silence
inside the tall cathedrals of sycamore and oak
as heretical crows streamed in to take over
the choir stalls and the sun ticked like a pendulum
between the trees which was why
I lay on the floor of the forest for hours
gazing up at the dissolving leaves as they
yellowed and reddened into legends of twilight

but it was for the sake of the sibyl
that I finally gave myself body and soul
to the mad destinies of smoke and wind
and it was for the sake of all my ruined reveries
breaking into soft blue light that I entered
the cave and waited with the sibyl for the echoes
of wild music to settle into one incessant note
that would stay in the head to torment us forever.

Judith Visits the Past

Already a century has passed since
the day when I left the Assyrian camp
and the moon's mystery saluted me
like a hooded woman.
I could feel manta rays roll
the ghostly hoops of their bodies
through darkening seas. Oh
I knew how pairs of eyes
flickered in the arched windows
as I approached that city of blue buildings,
imagining a crowded square with
jugglers tossing floodlit swords.

Now shadows are embracing
when I finally find the house
where I once lived as a widow.

With a push the heavy door moves,
Bethulia's gates suddenly swing open
and again I enter like a magician
lifting Holofernes' head from a sack
for the delighted people.

Yes, we won the war, my bold days ended,
and I returned to a life of fasting and prayer
in these rooms where others live.

But my own face stares from the tables.
My own body bursts from the walls.

Basket of Oranges

—after Matisse

I want the oranges in this basket
to stand for changes in my life.
I have embraced their floodtide of color—
I am letting it splash right over my body
like a blessing of ardent silk.
Alone in the darkened amphitheater
of my soul, I suddenly start to love
their gaiety, I begin to need
their brightness that sears silence
like a thousand live red coals.

I am keeping these green-leaved oranges
until I learn to live somehow
in their huge and ancient light,
as if I were a warrior on a white camel
crossing the sands of Morocco
under a hammered copper moon,
as if I were a merchant in the souks
placing the lucent globes of oranges
into baskets, greeting friends who pass
with kisses on the hair.

The Road to Sènanque

On the Sunday afternoon we entered
the canyon road to Sènanque, we were
feeding ourselves on daydreams, we were
wondering if this was our last trip to France
even as we craved the stern, hard-breathing beauty
of one more Cistercian abbey. If we were clothing
the memories of our youthful bodies
in bikinis and thongs instead of monastic gowns
it was because of the hot dry wind in Provence
or because of the scent of each other's groins on our fingertips
or because of the way our cremated ashes would sizzle
the day they hit the water. Lovely are
the thighs and shoulders of the monks still living
in seclusion at Sènanque, knotting the corners of their robes
before they walk in the wind and imagine themselves
wearing garments of owl feathers and pine.
To love beyond all measure: would we finally learn
what that means if we meditated on stone benches
and slept on straw beds on the floor, if we prayed,
planted lavender and cultivated honey, if we lost all courage
but stayed on the high narrow road to Sènanque?
Beautiful are your shoulders and your voice at the moment
when it first breaks the morning silence as we enter another day
to imagine ourselves traveling a blue, intimate void
chanting words that leave echoes like protective charms
and watch while the snow fills our door until
we feel ourselves become both mountain pass and sky.

Reading at Silvacane

In the silence she sits in a cloister reading. Her lips do not move.
Her gaze touches print like the sun skimming clouds.
A man wanders through the colonnade. He keeps moving.
She feels the set of his mouth, the tilted head, the taut hips.

Once a community of monks read here; a voice led them
through meals to Compline. Now she follows as the voice
leads her down the page; once read, the lines singe
and flute into smoke. Words disappear that way—
they vanish like shadows from the lime-washed walls.
Men disappear too when women keep them from moving.

Her hands do not move because they are veiled in words
steeped in silence to the core. As she listens, she can
hear the rhythmic strokes of a pen on parchment
(now fast, now slow) and she loses herself in the dark
swaying rows of lines (now thick, now thin).
The text erases; the silence floats, waiting to be read.

The monks at Silvacane did their work and prayed. At day's end
they sat on benches to chant psalms or they simply listened
to the voice of a reader reverberating through the room.
That voice recited through their nights and days as they
walked from one place to another—it moved them forward
slowly at one time until they became a single
melody reflected in cool, translucent glass.

Now the man sits alone on a bench inside the colonnade.
His most painful task is to touch her—nothing will change that.
His stillness is a path through which she enters the folded page.
A voice rises, syllables begin to crackle and burn
as a hand moves, assembling images on a screen:
the pulpit where a monk speaks in air dry as glass,
the cloister where a woman reads to find the miracle.

The Nuns of Alba

We had so much love for her,
more than the sisters at Avila.
We waited so long, but soon
our need to see her just once more
stilled our song at Matins,
spilled through our sleep. We knew
this convent was our tomb,
that we were corpses
as much as she. And always
that strong, sweet scent:
water of angels sprinkled
like perfume over our beds,
the same fragrance that kept
rising from her tomb,
a profusion of wild jasmine
that bloomed suddenly everywhere,
even deep inside the almonry.

We thought we could wait
forever, but without her we
were no more than live fish
lifted from the water:
we could not breathe.

So once more we entered the nave.
One by one we unfastened

glazed bricks. It took all night
to open the limestone wound.

We lifted her coffin's lid
and found there only
a cold, elegant marionette
stamped with cabouchons of earth,
and that mysterious fragrance
present still. We washed
the damp, delicate remains
with a light-headed pride,
we looked and looked at her
biting back our tender sighs
of hunger.

We had so much love for her.
For months after, we were as calm
as stunned puppets
locked inside the best dream
of our lives.

Mushrooms

Lounging
in a fruity haze
of mushrooms,
we have no strength
to cough or sneeze,
only to lie among
these cool, damp
parasols,
to let the horizon roll
into a slow meditation
of wood ash
and musky leaves,
to feel these children of darkness
breathe again
as they surround us
with the charmed scent
of almonds and wild mint,
their bodies shimmering
into a ring of sprites
spinning and diving
in a moonlit glade.
So when we pause
to sleep among them
we dance
with their enchanted fury,
wear velvet collars

and blind, milky eyes,
feel our bloodstreams rush
inside their waxy veins—
these foundlings of midnight!
It would be easy to find them
hushed and waiting
in an old apple orchard in Wales.
It would be easy to be good
if we were happy,
if we could spend our lives
veiled and perfumed
under their white umbrellas
glowing in the mist.
But overnight
the perfections of sorrow
spring up
inky and delicate
wherever our feet touched ground,
overnight we wake and become
the cold that rises
from these ghostly funnels
poison-crammed.

Syrinx

She was still trying to understand
the strangeness of her life—still remembered
his thin lips and pine-haunted brow,
her taut arm lifted behind her head
as if she could swim backward
through days already lived when a wild wind
came plunging through the grass and haze blued
at the river's edge like an unfamiliar fear
for it was too late to be herself—
to catch the eye of the pheasant
moving toward her with a slow swiveling strut,
too late to lose herself in the blaze of his head
tilted like a fringed ornament yet it
came back to her—the murmuring voice of Pan—
she remembered his inquisitive green-eyed stare,
his red hair flashing through the leaves as
she swayed and meditated inside the hollow reeds
where the veined and muscled dream of her body
kept straining for release into something real,
something finished and beautiful—
not this obstinacy of daylight nudging her from sleep,
not this tremolo spinning in her empty wrists
nor the giddy cantata in white fluttering
where words once frothed and burned
but now only flute notes turned in the air
the cold, clear music of birth and death
unbroken here in this eternal autumn.

A Walk through Soho

Other couples have made this journey,
I think to myself, as we face each other
linking arms like Eloise and Abelard
after a morning of silent sex.

Love writes hieroglyphs in ash.
Slowly I am learning to decipher this world
with your body, your unspoken words
the fast-falling tears I keep blinking back.

Passion is always its own rescue.
In the candlelit shop we enter someone plays
a bamboo flute, in the Thai restaurant you choose
I eat rice and imagine fire.

My poetics are a life you never made.
I am only the shadow of a heron
passing through your thoughts as
you turn to me smiling in mute daylight.

Dreamlife of a Mime

On the mountain, a hundred cloud shadows.
In her cup a single coin. Behind her eyes
the white stare of the soul.

Avignon. The Papal Palace Square.
Her eyes open the moment a coin clinks.
Wind sweeps down from the mountain.

Her body is a horse galloping
down streets she can almost recall.
The ground buckles. Pebbles spin.

Her grief is a horse. Galloping.

Each day she fasts from words.
She enters the silence as a temptress:
Salome unveiled.

When she slides the tube of elastic cloth over her body
her mood and gestures change.
Images obsess her.

Phantasms file toward her on the Papal Palace steps.
One smiles and stops to offer
his severed head as a lantern.

The tape recorder clicks.

Through the strains of an oboe
she cartwheels on the sun god's thigh
and feels the force of their duet.

She stretches toward him. Away from him.
His hands reshape her into a bowl.
As the moments pass.

As the bells chime lullabies. Elegies.

People pause to watch.
Human voices mean nothing.
Her arms slice air. Her torso bends.

Eruptions of change. Her knee rises.
Her fingers. Point to the sky.
Stasis in movement.

The oboe broods.

In the nuanced light her pelvis shifts.
She steps backward. Forward.
Desire is molded in the clay of her body.

A coin drops in the cup.

A camera whirs.

Yet the distance holds her.
Hunger floats and twirls
in the thousand gestures of a dream.

As the music slows.

As she wakes to remember herself.

Ariadne in Verona

To wander the ruined amphitheater
with a taste of tar in her mouth.
To sleep in a vacant square
as her marble bed grows softer.

To wake in a babble of hailstones
with unrelenting comraderie—with weariness.
To share at noon the anxious watch
of statues in a deserted garden.

To lift her arms because grief is spacious—
a plunge through the satins of Naxos!
To mark and slit the rustling bolts
into falling down days.

To sit alone and smoke until she finds
a pattern in the maze of myrtle
through which his restless body
drifts like a sleepwalker.

Black Coat

Your empty black coat
scented with almond
and old dollar bills
waits on the hanger
like a blameless exile
who has forgotten everything
except how to hug the dark.

Wherever I go, your skin's
piney fragrance remembers
to wash its bright wave
over my body. Each day
your heavy black coat
wears your weightless imprint
like the naked depth of a star.

I have folded myself into
your penumbra of silence,
have grown to know your
tender, essential way
of moving out into this life,
like the long black coat
that opens to warm you.

Bathsheba Bathing

Her heartbeat synchronizes with
the blink of two dispossessing eyes,

the dreams of Uriah filing through her blood
until she no longer can see herself.

Her bare body leans forward
hidden, exposed—

the torso like a face listening

as the words of a summons
palpitate in her hands
like gestures coiled inside a bud

or filaments of thought unwinding
to erase groin, nipples, brow.

She hears the whir of a spring
pulsing underground—

her own breath rising and falling
like clear deep water

while another gaze emerges
to glide down the surface of her body.

The letter drifts at her knees

and what is left unsaid
falls like light across the room,

then vanishes into the depth
of a meditation not yet begun.

After Abstinence

After years of abstinence
the humble shudders of orgasm.

She does not at first recall the sounds,
does not know if she is crying or laughing,
falling or regaining her balance,
drowning or swimming again,
her own voice rising in her ears
sings that delicate and brutal aria, yes
she knows it now, remembers how
the current rushes through her
sweeping the breath from
her throat in short, sweet gasps.

Pure, brief moment of life.

Then a gathering response: the echo
of her seaburst transfixed for an instant
before plunging into its own delight.

Winter night cold and black.
A wave from the past lifts her up
and crashes into its extinction.

Parmigianino Thinking

Lines perpetually slipping into dream—
in his mind they agitate like hands on water
tracing the grid of a shadowy cage.

And now they are here again—
two forms dancing, swirling, laughing,
unscrolling into ribbons of pen and wash.

They descend to circle each other,
tilt their heads and join hands
that atomize into a cloud of red chalk.

A wand lifts and moves out over space
retracing the gestures of shoulders and limbs
lingering in their own transparencies.

Two bodies coalesce not once but twice
and rise like dark quivering trees,
their branches woven with blossoms of silk.

Like ancestral ghosts they flutter in the air
or maidens whose heads bear baskets
of olives, figs, and wine.

They flow far back into themselves
through rivers that unendingly reflect
the movements of their dance.

Through leaves, shadows, a blue-violet sky,
their yearning contours pale to dissolve
and then come gliding back

into a tender paraphrase of reeds
gathered in the wind's distracted sway—
lines leaving only to return.

Sister-in-law

Her cheek pressed to my cheek,
her brother my husband
enthroned in a palace of dust.

Her unforgiving eyes
sweep through our shared past
of rung bells, children born
and let the moody doves
resettle in the scorched trees.

The first time she looked at me
her gaze was milder than
wind genuflecting on water
but then the breathless shadows
of her suspicion thickened,
the lake dried and raised
its hidden grotto of stones.

Now her walk is stooped,
her hair a thin white sleep.
Her eyes roam not toward me
but somewhere beyond sea and stars.

Her face hardens, the eyeholes empty
and again she is lost
in the unrelenting light of a form
taking root and vanishing.

Centaur's Blood

When at last Rumor came panting into Deianira's room
and four separate letters slammed into
one awful whole—IOLE—she felt the river's force
again sweeping through her, the voice
of Nessus came rushing back over her—
to help make him love you—only this time
she knew herself truly abandoned when
the water rose over her lips eyes hair

yet it was then she remembered the charm still
there locked away—to help make him love you—
and her grief caught in a smoke as blue and strange
as the centaur's blood—syllables whispered
over a vial of myrrh—the words inscribed themselves
on every part of her body—*to help make him love you*

and the creature rose galloping through continents of ash
blinding her, leading her to the plunge of hooves into water
and a man's arms lifting her to his chest—
then the gods blinked an arrow whirred
and the centaur's dream settled over her shoulders
like a mantle of crimson shadow that she folded
and placed now in Rumor's hands to give to Heracles.

For she had only done what the centaur said,
what the sparks sang as they scattered on the hearth
from a fire flickering white yellow blue—
all night she watched and listened, her thoughts
tumbling in bubbles of flame water blood.

On the Appian Way

When I reached the Tomb of Cecilia Metella
along the road lined with cypresses
and the timbre of the custodian's greeting
was the sting of your radiance in my veins,

when I looked beyond the walls into open fields
and deciphered in the cryptic markings
of parasol pines a code for passion
signified outside the forms of flesh,

when I stood with other travelers
under ruined stone arches to hear the custodian
praise the love of Metellus for Cecilia—
"dispossessed, she was his only possession,"—

the burnt eloquence of words—
so much a part of you—returned
and line by line I began to read
that book of smoke your illness.

Pythia: The Process

First the slow ease of weightlessness,
then her lifted body woven
into a cold chrysalis of fern.

Next the spiced scent of burnt laurel,
then a secret smoke of barley and pine
ghosting from a cleft in stone.

Now again the ice gleam of wings—
the melting pull of translucent butterflies
moving her to a tripod,

now the bleating sacrificial goat,
then her own limbs trembling as
the freezing pin-pricks of Apollo's voice

sprinkled through her organs
and breathed her out of herself
into a dim beat of thrown pebbles—

into the pulse of words.
Again she bent over a bowl of clear water
as it whitened into foam—

the particles of time dissolved
into a thunder of before now after
rising from the temple floor.

Then the priest spoke and trance
released her, breath by breath.
Then her own music began.

Mind Clearing in a Chinese Landscape

I am ready to go far into the mountains
to wear my rag robe and live at the foot of a tree.
I will sleep sitting up and wear the jewel
of eros like a hoof print in my forehead
and stand under the drip ledge of an old stone cave
to bid the craving self a cool farewell.

For years I drifted invisibly through blizzards
of coal dust and snow—I was the electric wire
chanting snatches from an isolate tune rising
somewhere behind the backwater of a place
where the spirits were strong in winter
and pain floated like a sacred thread over my shoulder.

But when the moon tattooed a dot of saffron light
on my cheek and the past vanished
like a lit candle lowered into water,
I wrapped my torn sandals and rusted kettle
into a blanket that I folded like a lotus
so my bones would dream of flowers.

And the music surrounded me—
the rhythms of timbrels, bells, and drums
turned my head toward the east
where mist unfolded and bloomed like japonica
along the meditation path that would take me
from trees and mountains into clouds.

Now I will follow the fragrance of blossoms
and old books, not pausing to look back
when sadness drizzles ash on my tongue.
I hold a twig of goldleaf, for contemplation,
in one hand and carry a silver coin in the other
to place in my mouth as I cross the river.

Made in the USA
Lexington, KY
21 November 2009